SAN DIEGO
PADRES

STARS, STATS, HISTORY, AND MORE!

BY JIM GIGLIOTTI

The Child's World®
childsworld.com

Published by The Child's World®
1980 Lookout Drive • Mankato, MN 56003-1705
800-599-READ • www.childsworld.com

ISBN 9781503828360
LCCN 2018944850

Printed in the United States of America
PAO2392

Photo Credits:
Cover: AP Images/Samuel Stringer/Icon Sportswire;
(inset) Joe Robbins.
Inside: AP Images: David Durochik 9, Denis Poroy 17, Will
Powers 19, Kynsung Gong 24; Dreamstime.com: Jerry
Coli 5, 23, Alan Crosthwaite 13, Ivansabo 14, Keeton10
20; Newscom: Adam Bowl/Icon NC 10, Alan Smith/Icon
DHM 27; Joe Robbins: 6, 29.

About the Author

Jim Gigliotti has worked for
the University of Southern
California's athletic
department, the Los Angeles
Dodgers, and the National
Football League. He is now an
author who has written more
than 80 books, mostly for
young readers, on a variety
of topics.

On the Cover

Main photo: First baseman
Eric Hosmer;
Inset: hitting legend Tony Gwynn

CONTENTS

GO, PADRES!

The story of the Padres features outfielder Tony Gwynn. He was a great hitter and the best player in team history. He is in the Hall of Fame. But Gwynn retired in 2001. Today's Padres are trying to make their own history. They have good young players who have come up through the team's **minor leagues**. They hope to bring the Padres their first title!

Tony Gwynn's sweet swing helped him win eight NL batting titles. ➤

WHO ARE THE PADRES?

he Padres play in the National League (NL). That group is part of Major League Baseball (MLB). MLB also includes the American League (AL). There are 30 teams in MLB. The winner of the NL plays the winner of the AL in the **World Series**. The Padres have finished the season in first place five times. They have won the NL **pennant** twice.

◄ *José Pirela has seen action at first base, second base, and third base for the Padres.*

WHERE THEY CAME FROM

The Padres started playing in 1969. They were an expansion team. That means they were a new team that started from scratch. MLB wanted to grow bigger. The Padres got their name from a minor-league team in San Diego. *Padre* means "father" or "priest" in Spanish. Priests from Spain formed the first **mission** in San Diego in 1769.

First baseman Steve Garvey helped the ➤
Padres win the NL West in 1984.

WHO THEY PLAY

The Padres play 162 games each season. They play 81 games at home and 81 on the road. Some of their games are against other California teams. Like the Padres, the Los Angeles Dodgers and the San Francisco Giants play in the NL West Division. The Arizona Diamondbacks and the Colorado Rockies are also in the division. Teams play more games against their own division than any other division.

◄ *Freddy Galvis slides in safely below the tag of a Diamondbacks player.*

WHERE THEY PLAY

The Padres play at Petco Park. The stadium is **unique**. It has an old warehouse down the left-field line. The foul pole is painted right on the building! Fans can sit outside the warehouse. They can eat and shop inside it. Petco Park also has a grassy area beyond the outfield wall. Kids play out there while the big guys are playing on the field. It's a park within a park!

At Petco Park, fans sit in seats attached to the ➤ front of an old warehouse building.

THE BASEBALL FIELD

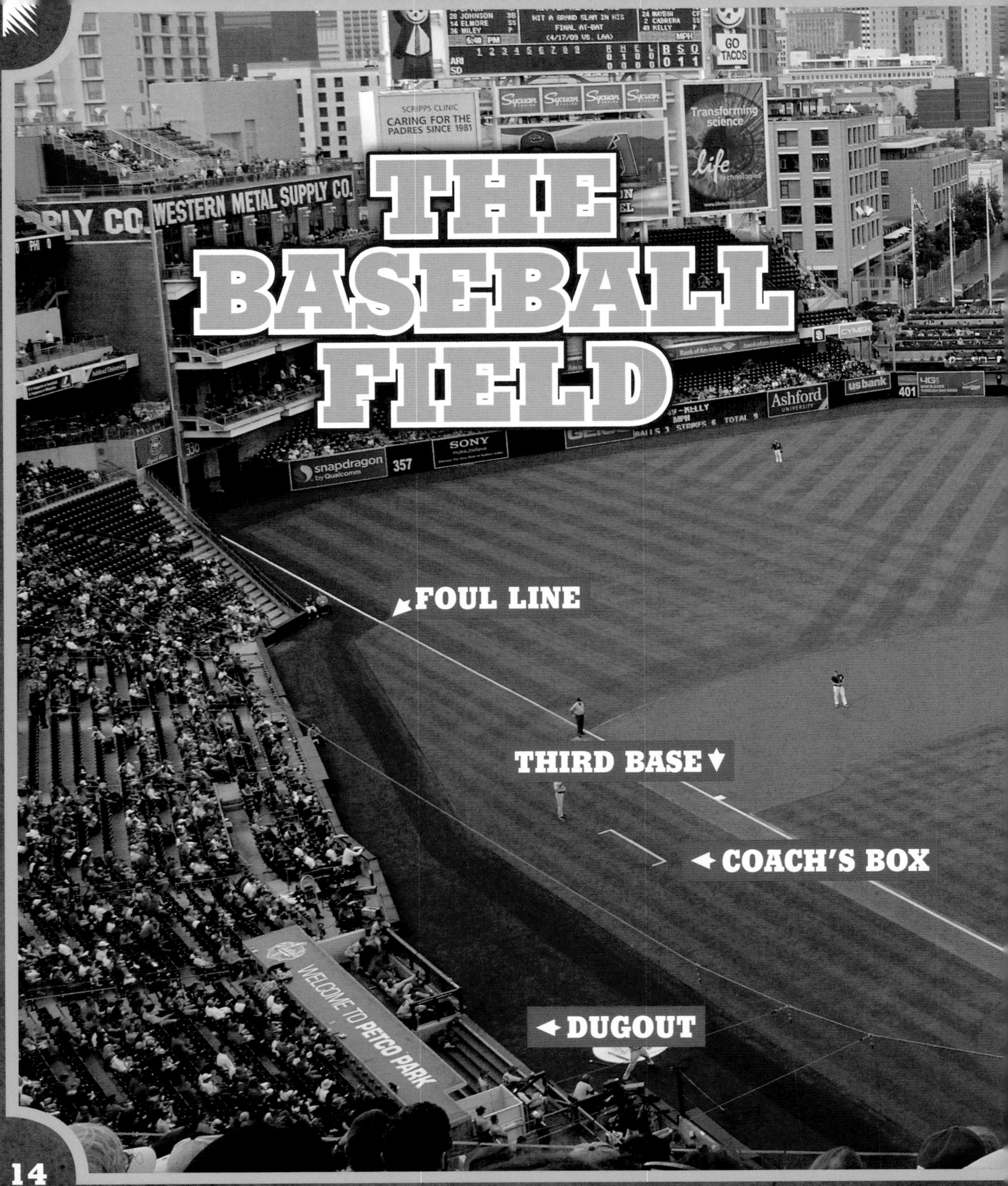

← FOUL LINE

THIRD BASE ▼

← COACH'S BOX

← DUGOUT

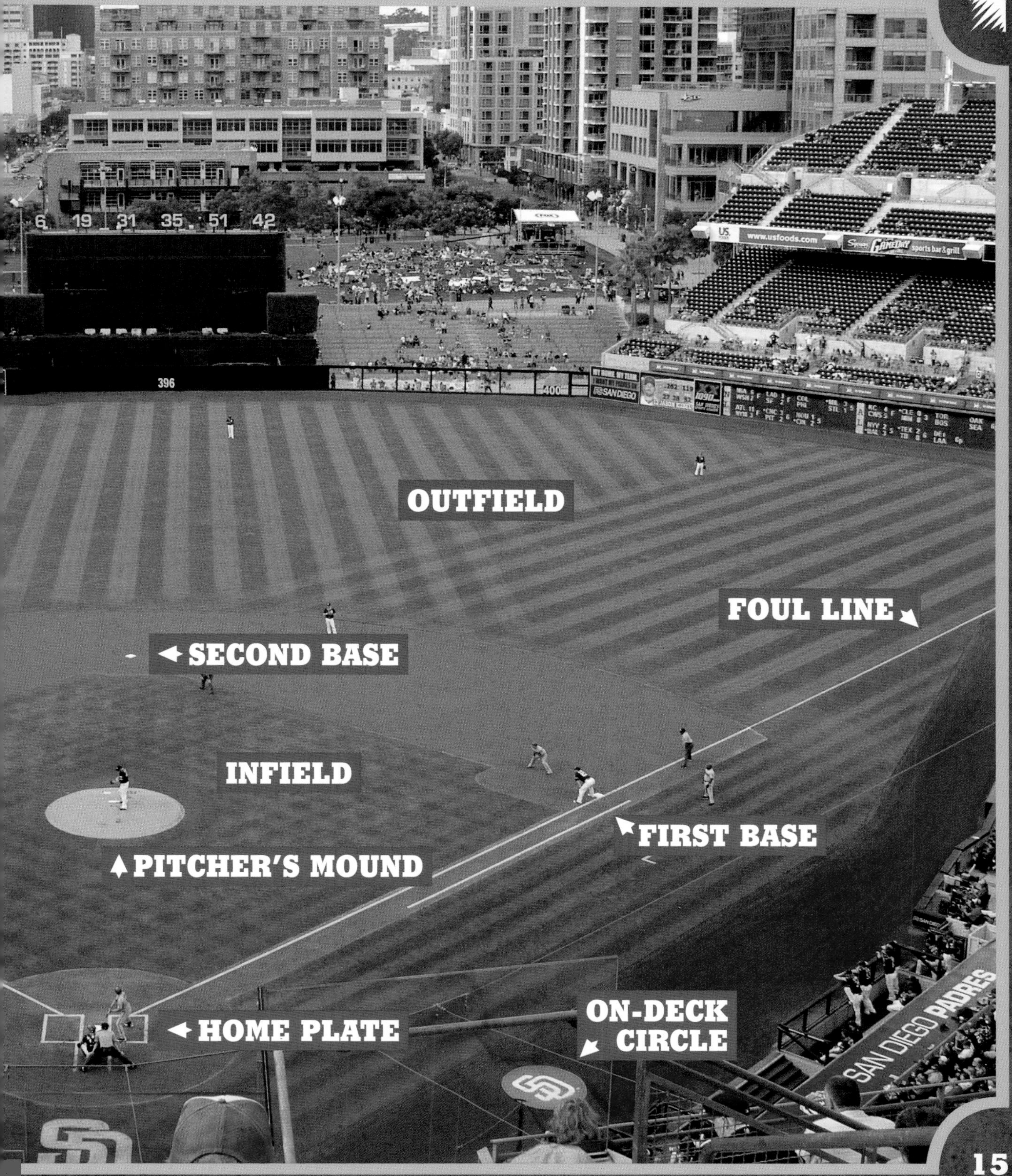

OUTFIELD

FOUL LINE

◄ SECOND BASE

INFIELD

FIRST BASE

▲ PITCHER'S MOUND

ON-DECK CIRCLE

◄ HOME PLATE

BIG DAYS

Padres fans always remember Steve Garvey's home run in the 1984 **playoffs**. His ninth-inning hit beat the Chicago Cubs 7–5. The next day, the Padres won their first pennant. Here are a few other big days in team history.

1972—Nate Colbert had one of the best hitting days in history. It came in a doubleheader at Atlanta. In Game 1, the Padres first baseman hit two home runs and drove in five runs. In Game 2, he had three homers and eight RBI! The Padres won both games.

Trevor Hoffman waves to fans after setting a ➤ new MLB saves record in 2006.

1996—Tony Gwynn's brother Chris had a big day. He hit a two-run double in the eleventh inning. The Padres beat the Dodgers 2–0. The big hit gave the Padres the division title.

2006—The Padres beat the Pirates 2–1 late in the season. It was key to helping the Padres win the division. Trevor Hoffman got the **save**. It was the 479th of his career. That set a new MLB record.

TOUGH DAYS

Every MLB team has some tough days in its history. Here are a few Padres fans would like to forget.

1970—Clay Kirby had a **no-hitter** after eight innings against the Mets. But the Padres were losing 1–0. The Mets had scored on a groundout. Kirby was taken out for a pinch-hitter. The Mets got three hits in the ninth. They won 3–0.

2007—The Padres and Rockies tied for the last NL playoff spot. So they had a playoff to see which team made the playoffs! The Rockies won 9–8 in 13 innings.

2018—The Padres' home park is less than 20 miles from Mexico. The Padres wanted to impress their fans south of the border in a series in Mexico. They played the Dodgers in Monterrey, Mexico. But the Dodgers won 4–0. The Padres didn't get a hit!

▼ *A Rockies player slides home with a run in the Padres' 2007 loss.*

MEET THE FANS!

The San Diego area includes almost one million members of the military and their families. Some of them are still in the Navy or Army. Some of them are retired. Many of them are Padres fans! The team honors the military at every Sunday home game. The players wear special uniforms. The fans come to the games in their service uniforms.

◄ *Padres players wear camouflage uniforms in honor of the U.S. military.*

HEROES THEN

There's no bigger hero in Padres history than Tony Gwynn. He was a hitting machine. He batted .338 in his career. He was an All-Star 15 times. He played all 20 of his seasons in San Diego. The fans loved him for that! Dave Winfield and Nate Colbert were top sluggers. Trevor Hoffman was a great **closer**. Hoffman is in the Hall of Fame.

Dave Winfield began his Hall of Fame career in San Diego. ➤

HEROES NOW

Outfielder Wil Myers has power and speed. First baseman Eric Hosmer joined the Padres in 2018. He was an All-Star in Kansas City. He helped the Royals win the World Series in 2015. Clayton Richards leads the pitching staff. Joey Lucchesi is a San Diego pitcher to watch in the future.

 Wil Myers shows off his great batting stroke.

GEARING UP

Baseball players wear team uniforms. On defense, they wear leather gloves to catch the ball. As batters, they wear hard helmets. This protects them from pitches. Batters hit the ball with long wood bats. Each player chooses his own size of bat. Catchers have the toughest job. They wear a lot of protection.

THE BASEBALL

The outside of the Major League baseball is made from cow leather. Two leather pieces shaped like 8s are stitched together. There are 108 stitches of red thread. These stitches help players grip the ball. Inside, the ball has a small center of cork and rubber. Hundreds of feet of yarn are tightly wound around this center.

CATCHER'S
HELMET ➤

◄ CHEST
PROTECTOR

CATCHER'S
◄ MASK

WRIST BANDS ➤

CATCHER'S
MITT ➤

SHIN GUARDS ➤

CATCHER'S GEAR

TEAM STATS

ere are some of the all-time career records for the San Diego Padres. All of these stats are through the 2018 regular season.

HOME RUNS

Nate Colbert	163
Adrian Gonzalez	161

STOLEN BASES

Tony Gwynn	319
Gene Richards	242

BATTING AVERAGE

Tony Gwynn	.338
Mark Loretta	.314

STRIKEOUTS

Jake Peavy	1,348
Andy Benes	1,036

WINS

Eric Show	100
Randy Jones, Jake Peavy	92

SAVES

Trevor Hoffman	552
Heath Bell	134

Tony Gwynn is also the Padres all-time leader ➤ in games, at-bats, and walks.

RBI	
Tony Gwynn	1,138
Dave Winfield	626

GLOSSARY

closer (KLOH-zer) in baseball, a relief pitcher whose job it is to protect his team's lead in a game

minor leagues (MY-ner LEEGZ) pro baseball organizations below the level of Major League Baseball

mission (MISH-un) a local church built for the purpose of telling more people about a religion

no-hitter (noh-HIT-er) a game in which one team does not get any base hits

pennant (PEN-nunt) a thin, pointed flag; it represents the winning team in the AL or NL each year

playoffs (PLAY-offs) games played between top teams to determine who moves ahead

save (SAYV) in baseball, a statistic that indicates a pitcher has successfully preserved his team's win

unique (you-NEEK) special; one-of-a-kind

World Series (WURLD SEE-reez) the championship of Major League Baseball, played between the winners of the AL and NL

FIND OUT MORE

IN THE LIBRARY

Jacobs, Greg. *The Everything Kids' Baseball Book: 10th Edition.* New York, NY: Adams Media, 2018.

Mugford, Simon. *Baseball Superstars 2018: Facts & Stats.* New York, NY: Carlton Books, 2018.

Sports Illustrated Kids (editors). *Baseball: Then to Wow!* New York, NY: Sports Illustrated Kids, 2016.

ON THE WEB

Visit our website for links about the San Diego Padres: **childsworld.com/links**

Note to Parents, Teachers, and Librarians: We routinely verify our Web links to make sure they are safe and active sites. So encourage your readers to check them out!

INDEX